VAN GOGH MUSEUM AMSTERDAM

HIGHLIGHTS OF THE COLLECTION

MARKO KASSENAAR

Edited by
LIESBETH HEENK

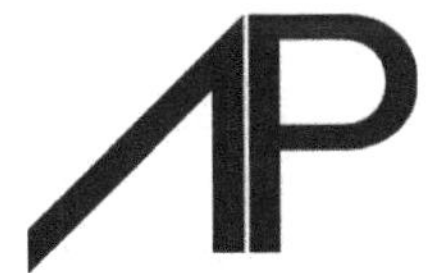

Publisher: Amsterdam Publishers, The Netherlands

ISBN 13: 9789492371386 (ebook)

ISBN 13: 9789492371379 (paperback)

CONTENTS

INTRODUCTION

In this guide you will be introduced to Van Gogh's masterpieces, and you will discover some of the ideas and ambitions behind his art.

This comprehensive guide to the Van Gogh museum's holdings provides the ideal introduction to the masterpieces from one of the world's most popular and beloved museums. For the purpose of clarity we will stick to a chronological presentation, while discussing works by Van Gogh and by other artists separately.

The Van Gogh museum houses the world's largest Van Gogh collection, comprising some 200 paintings, 400 drawings and 700 letters.

On display along with these works are masterpieces by Van Gogh's contemporaries, including Paul Gauguin, Emile Bernard, Georges Seurat, Camille Pissarro, Paul Signac and Auguste Rodin.

When Vincent van Gogh died in 1890, he did not leave a will. The artist's three sisters Elisabeth, Anna and Willemien decided that all of Van Gogh's work would be inherited by Theo, who after all took care of him during his entire career. Thus, the entire collection of Van

Gogh paintings, drawings and letters were owned by Van Gogh's brother Theo.

After Theo's death, on 25 January 1891, it passed to his widow, Johanna van Gogh-Bonger (1862-1925). She sold some of the works, but the majority stayed in her possession and were inherited by her son, Vincent Willem van Gogh (1890-1978) in 1925. Part of the works she sold are now in the wonderful collection of the Kröller-Müller museum in The Netherlands. This museum, set in a beautiful park, holds the second largest collection of Van Goghs in the world, and is definitely worthwhile a visit.

Vincent, an engineer, loaned some of his uncle's works to the Stedelijk Museum, Amsterdam's premier venue for modern art, in 1930. As the appreciation for the works of the artist Vincent van Gogh exploded, the demand grew for a special museum. At that time, a museum dedicated to a single artist was still something of an anomaly.

A foundation was set up in order to keep Van Gogh's unsold paintings and drawings, but also other artists' work as well as the book and print collections, together as one collection. Various paintings by Van Gogh's friends and contemporaries were part of the collection of contemporary art owned by Vincent and his brother Theo van Gogh.

In 1962, the collection was put in the care of the foundation for 15 million guilders, even though the estimated value of the collection was more than 300 million guilders.

The Dutch state built the Van Gogh Museum and still acts as the collection's administrator. Legally, the collection is on permanent loan to the Dutch state.

In 1973 Queen Juliana of the Netherlands opened the Van Gogh Museum, housed in the same specially designed building that it occupies today.

The collection has substantially grown since the inauguration of the museum, and through the financial support of the Vincent van Gogh Foundation, the Prince Bernhard Fund and many other sponsors, new works of exceptional standing have been acquired. The museum regularly exhibits long-term loans from other institutions.

THE BUILDING

The original museum building is designed by one of the most prominent members of the Dutch artistic movement *De Stijl*, the architect Gerrit Rietveld.

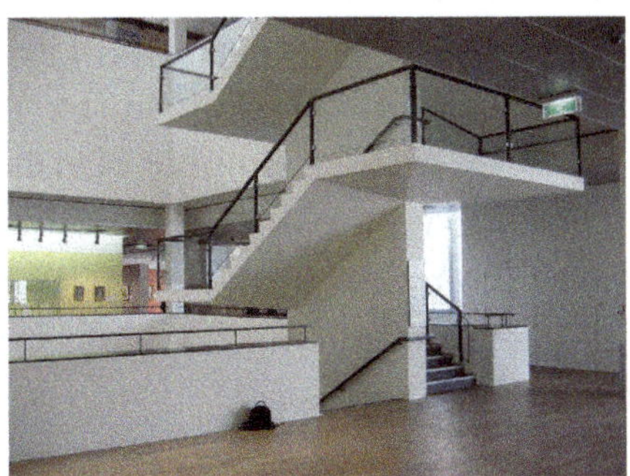

Japanese Wing of the Van Gogh Museum, main building., designed by Gerrit Rietveld. Photography by Minke Wagenaar – Wikimedia Commons.

Unfortunately, Rietveld was not able to fully realize his vision, as he died before the completion of the building in 1973. Still, with its clear lines and walls devoid of embellishment, enabling the visitor to focus entirely on the paintings themselves, the Van Gogh Museum is characteristic of Rietveld who was famous for his simplified creations.

The annex was designed by the architect Kisho Kurokawa (1934 - 2007) and built in 1999. It is known as the Kurokawa wing, and is used for temporary exhibitions.

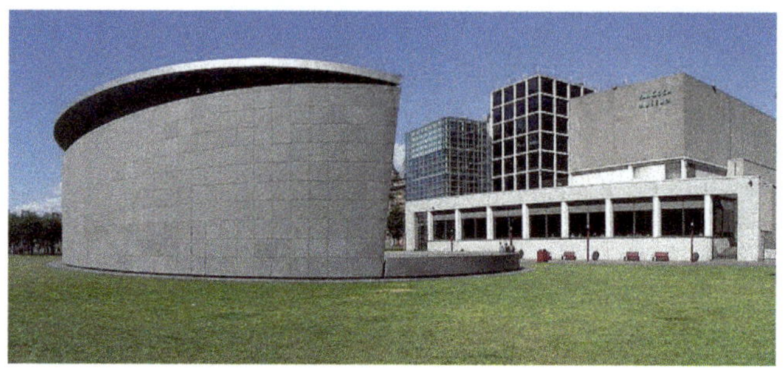

The Kurokawa wing of the Van Gogh Museum. Photography by Wladislav – Wikimedia Commons.

More recent alterations to the building include the construction of a new entrance hall. Since September 2015, visitors enter the museum through a glass building on Museumplein. The new transparent structure gave the museum another 800 square meters, improving the experience for the ever growing number of visitors. . Due to time-slotted admission tickets, visitor do not perceive the museum as overcrowded, even in the rather busy summer months. There is a new spacious and light reception area with cloakrooms, and a completely redesigned museum shop.

Having long been a dream of the museum, the new entrance hall was designed by Kisho Kurokawa Architect & Associates from Tokyo, the same agency that worked on the annex.

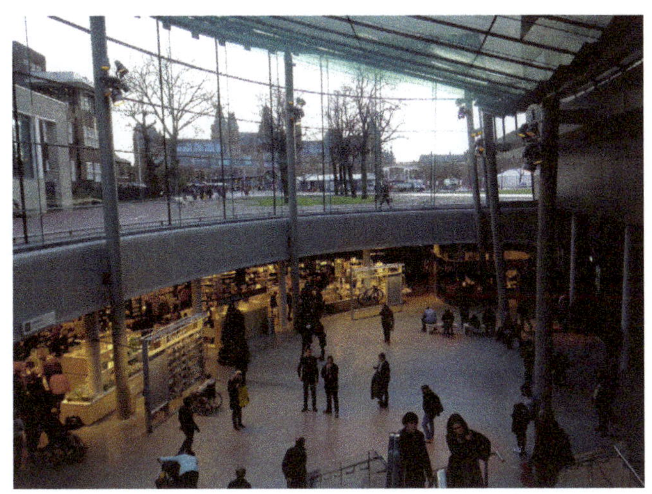

Interior of the new entrance hall with the Rijksmuseum in the back. Photograph by the author.

The Van Gogh Museum is one of the most popular museums in Amsterdam. In 2016 the total number of visitor was more than 2 million, coming from over 125 countries in the world, The majority of visitors were from the Netherlands, followed by the United States, Italy, France and Great Britain.

SHORT BIOGRAPHY OF VINCENT VAN GOGH

When comparing Vincent van Gogh's career with those of other artists, it soon becomes clear that his was one of the shortest in art history. It was not until the age of twenty-seven that he began work as a full-time professional painter, and he died a mere ten years later.

Yet in this short window of time, Vincent van Gogh (1853 - 1890) produced a body of works that is not only impressive in size, but also marks the origin of several modern art movements.

From the years following his death up until present day, artists have been inspired by his vibrant and innovative use of color, his expressionism, as well as his uncompromising attitude towards art and life.

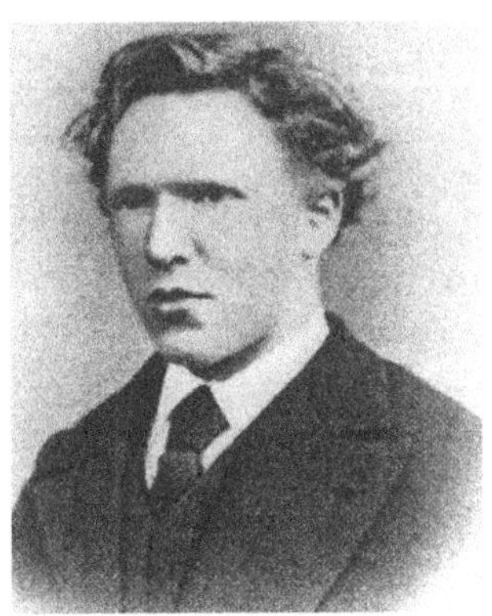

Vincent van Gogh, 18 years old.

Born in the small town of Groot-Zundert (Brabant) in The Netherlands in 1853, Vincent Willem van Gogh was a shy and introverted child. At the age of sixteen he began work as an assistant at the art dealership Goupil & Co. in The Hague, a company his brother Theo would also join a few years later.

During this time, Van Gogh was reassigned to various major cities including London and Paris, before eventually losing his job in 1876. Although he loved art, he did not especially like his job in the art world. After his dismissal, he took an unpaid job at a boarding school in Ramsgate (England). Various other jobs followed, not terribly successful. In 1878 he relocated to Belgium to work as a layman minister, and ended up realizing his artistic calling.

Van Gogh's career properly began in 1880, after he had moved back to The Netherlands where he hoped to find work as an illustrator for magazines and newspapers.

The first years were difficult and consisted of endless studying and copying prints. Unfortunately he lacked an innate talent, so it took considerable time before he could draw properly; Van Gogh was incapable of drawing 'from nature'. He needed an object in front of him, but even then, the result was awkward. More often than not the postures of his figures were rather wooden, with arms and legs being out of proportion.

The Hague period saw some touching drawings of figures, and the highlight of his Dutch years, *The Potato Eaters,* was made in Nuenen (Brabant) in 1885. After a short period of studying art in Antwerp, Van Gogh decided to go to Paris to live with his brother, who had by then become manager of Goupil & Co.

It was in Paris that Van Gogh developed the personal style that would epitomize his work. Influenced by impressionism, he experimented with vivid colors and expressive brushstrokes, and he also discovered a new source of inspiration in the plethora of Japanese art that was entering the capital at this time.

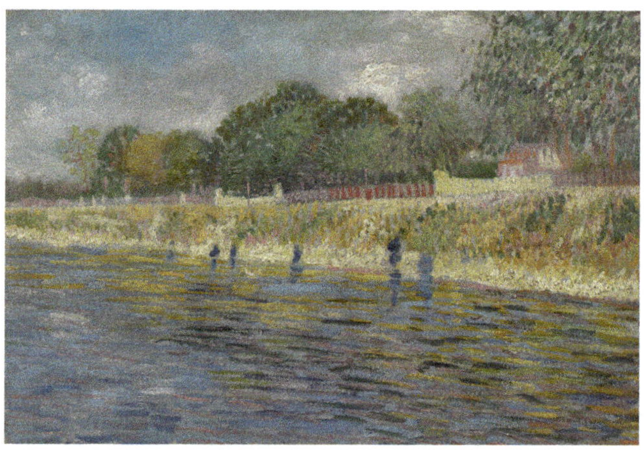

Vincent van Gogh, Bank of the Seine, oil on canvas, May - July 1887

Noise, temptation and the bustle of city life began took their toll on Van Gogh. Anxious, stressed and in the early stages of alcoholism, he escaped to the tranquillity of Arles in southern France. The artist also hoped that life would be less expensive in the country. It was in Arles that he painted his most iconic works, such as *The Sunflowers* and his own bedroom in the Yellow House.

Already suffering from a deteriorating mental illness, Van Gogh began to experience epileptic seizures. Living together with Paul Gauguin in the Yellow House in Arles ended in disaster; in December 1888 he dramatically cut off his left ear and was hospitalized.

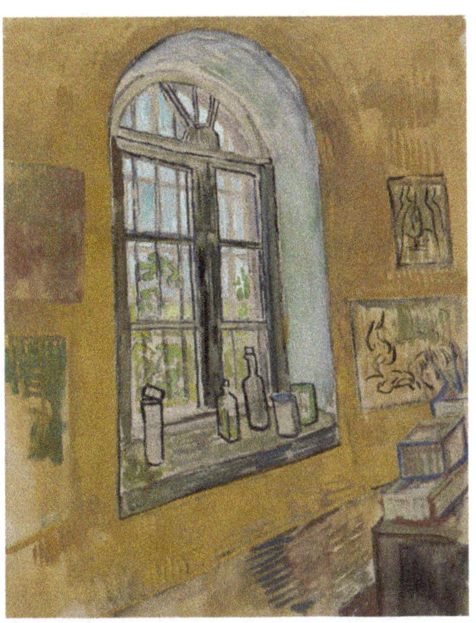

Vincent van Gogh, Window in the Studio, mixed media on paper, September – October 1889

The unique discovery of a doctor's letter containing information about the cut-off ear aroused great interest in 2016. It showed that he did not simply cut off an earlobe, as was hitherto thought, but his entire ear.

The combination of his illness and fierce temper meant that the villagers began to fear him. The artist felt he was unable to live on his own, and volunteered to be admitted to an asylum in Saint-Rémy.

He stayed in the asylum of Saint-Paul for two years where he was allowed to work in an empty room that he used as studio. It was a period of great distress; he had various epileptic seizures and he feared that the time would eventually come that he would be unable to paint or draw. That, of course, was his biggest fear. At the same time it was also a period during which his star began to rise; articles about Van Gogh's work were starting to appear. Upon being released from the asylum, Van Gogh moved to Auvers-sur-Oise, near Paris. There, the local Dr. Gachet would look after him.

In this village, Van Gogh painted his final works before his tragic death on 29th July 1890. Dying from a bullet wound to the chest, it seems plausible that Van Gogh shot himself. The revolver with which Van Gogh seems to have fatally wounded himself was found in Auvers in 2016.

Buried in Auvers-sur-Oise, Van Gogh was not alone for long, since his brother Theo came to share his resting place only six months later.

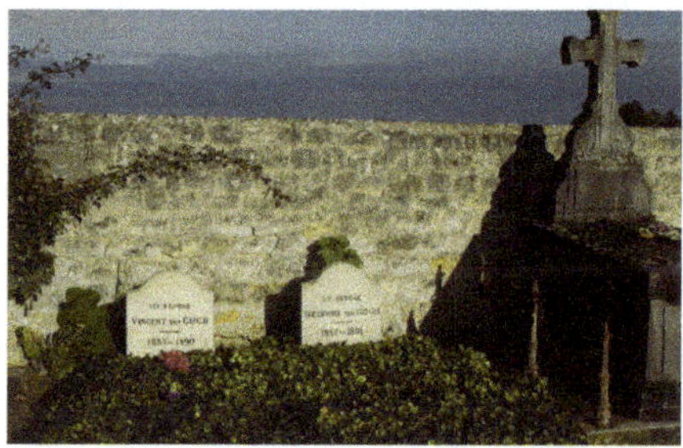

The graves of Vincent van Gogh and Theo van Gogh in Auvers-sur-Oise

PERMANENT COLLECTION

In November 2014 the Van Gogh Museum redesigned the presentation of its permanent collection, putting more emphasis on what draws people from all over the world to the museum: the artist's tortured life.

The museum nowadays focuses on the complete story: the artist, the context, Van Gogh's personal ambitions, his emotions, the many myths and his influence on other artists.

If you enter the museum you will be face to face with larger than life blow-ups of the artist's multi-colored self-portrait and half a dozen of painted self-portraits. This is the right choice: we, the public, are very much interested in getting to know the man Van Gogh.

In the presentation Van Gogh's paintings have been given ample space, and the walls vary in color. They have chosen a greyish-brown for the early Brabant paintings and drawings, a green-blue for the Paris pictures, a rich blue for his dazzling works from Provence, and various subtle greens and blues for his other works. Because of the fragility of works on paper, a changing selection of only a few drawings are being displayed.

Although the display is basically chronological, the work has been arranged according to certain themes. As a visitor you can follow the on-going search of this extraordinary artist. Issues are being discussed such as the ear incident, the suicide and the mental illness, death and recognition, the discoloration of his paintings and the origins of the Van Gogh museum. At the very end of the presentation, on the top floor of the building, a gallery displays work by Van Gogh's followers.

THE NETHERLANDS

Not only is *The Potato Eaters* considered the artist's first masterpiece, it is also the largest work he ever painted. It portrays a peasant family, illuminated by a single lamp, with nothing except potatoes to eat for their dinner.

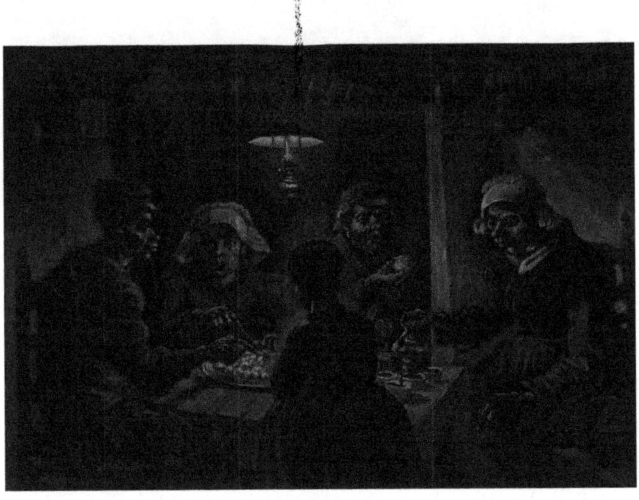

Vincent van Gogh, The Potato Eaters, oil on canvas, April - May 1885

To the right, a woman pours chicory, a cheap substitute for coffee. The hardened faces and muted colors suggest the burdens of life in the countryside.

By looking closely, one can make out a clock alongside a painting of the crucifixion in the background on the upper left. You may not see this on the reproduction, but you'll notice it in the museum.

Affected by his time as a lay preacher amongst the poor in the Borinage mining district of Belgium, Van Gogh was deeply sympathetic to the sufferings of common people.

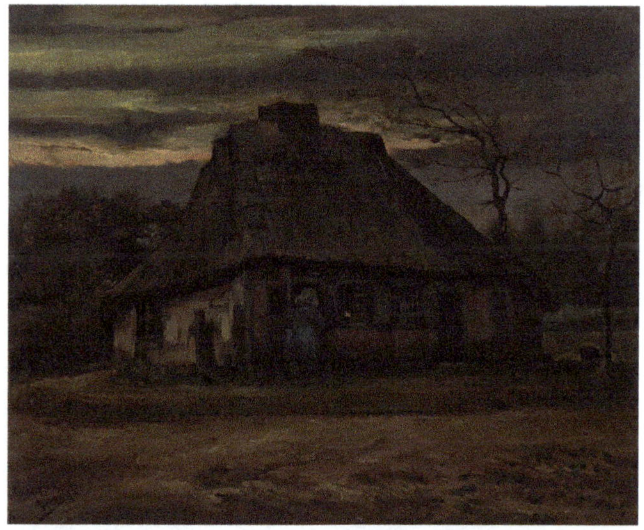

Vincent van Gogh, The cottage, oil on canvas, May 1885

The artist wrote to his brother Theo on 30 April 1885 that the painting had to express the idea that these farmers:

> "tilled the earth themselves with these hands they are putting in the dish, (...) and that they have thus honestly *earned* their food."

Using farmers and laborers as his models, like Jules Breton and Jean-

François Millet had done before him, the countryside was his preferred setting and subject. *The Potato Eaters* forms part of a series of works on this theme, using the dark colors that were popular in the Netherlands during this time.

ANTWERP (1885 - 1886)

Having employed dark, sombre colors for the majority of his early works, Van Gogh decided to brighten his palette and began to take courses at the art academy in Antwerp.

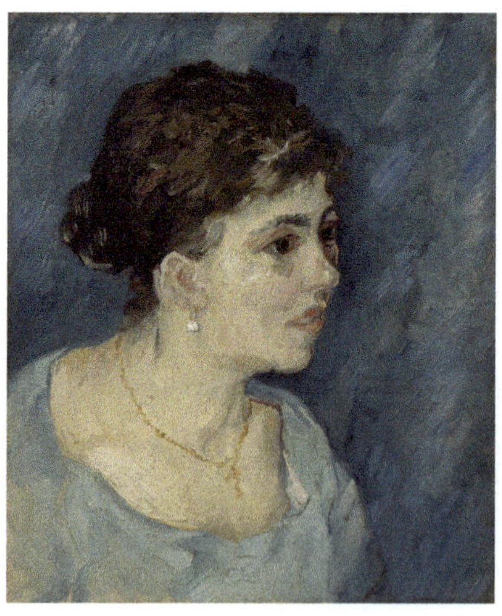

Vincent van Gogh, Portrait of a Prostitute, oil on canvas, December 1885

The colors went from muted browns and grays to vibrant blues and rosy skin, and the brushstrokes became more refined.

Remaining poor throughout his life, Van Gogh often hired prostitutes, like the woman in this portrait, to sit for his paintings rather than professional models since they demanded a significantly lower fee.

As his art earned him no money, Van Gogh found himself financially dependent on his brother Theo. Theo fully supported him from 1882 onwards, agreeing that this arrangement would remain in place until the artist could support himself. This would never happen. (Cf *Van Gogh and Money. The Myth of the Poor Artist* by Liesbeth Heenk.)

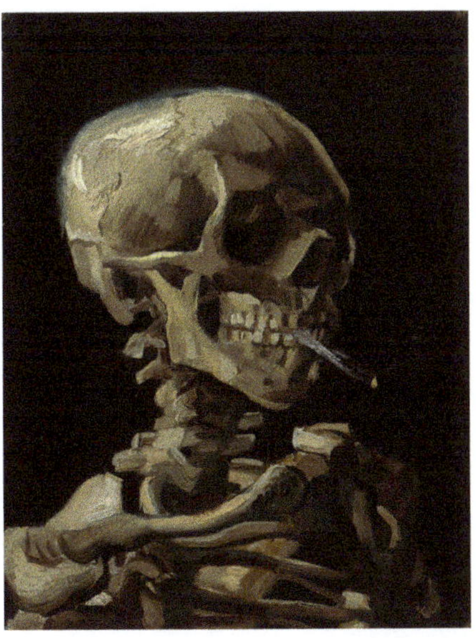

Vincent van Gogh, Head of a skeleton with a burning cigarette, oil on canvas, February 1886

The *Head of a skeleton with a burning cigarette*, made in February 1886, is probably an ironic comment on the traditional training offered at the Antwerp academy where Van Gogh enrolled for a short course, and where he was criticized for painting 'too roughly'.

A skeleton would often be used in class to study human anatomy. Van Gogh used this familiar subject to make his own wry statement.

PARIS (1886 - 1888)

Paris signified a new life for Van Gogh. New influences from art movements like impressionism and pointillism transformed his way of working. The rough brushstrokes from his earlier Dutch works were replaced by dots and small stripes, and he used much lighter colors.

Like other Parisian painters of this period, Van Gogh painted people in natural settings, such as parks and gardens. This painting uses an old-fashioned composition as a model: the horizon is placed in the middle of the canvas, with one tree positioned exactly in the centre, and a pair of lovers depicted on either side.

Though this is not yet the work of an avant-garde artist such as his contemporaries Gauguin or Bernard, the magnificent colors reveal Van Gogh's development.

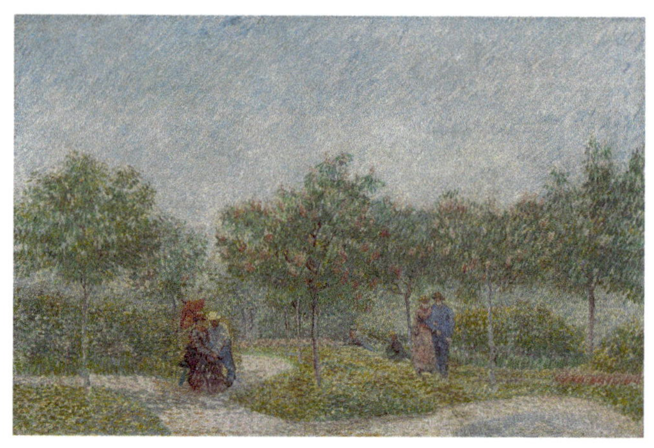

Vincent van Gogh, Garden with Courting Couples: Square Saint-Pierre, oil on canvas, May 1887

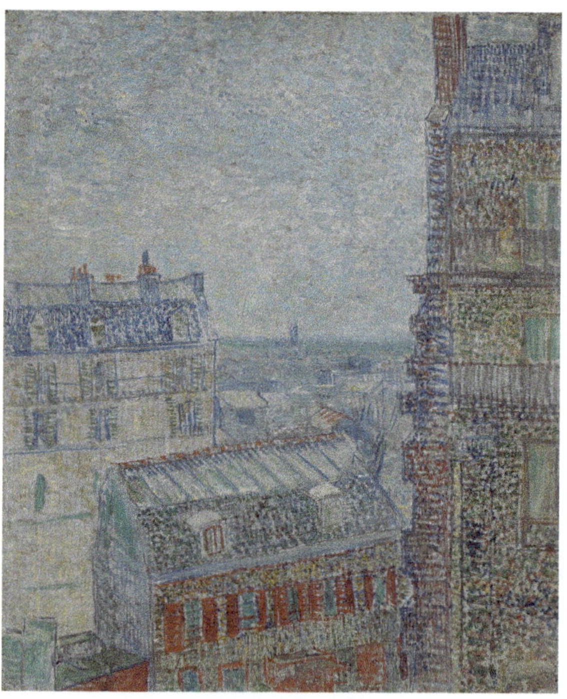

Vincent van Gogh, View from Theo's apartment, oil on canvas, March - April 1887

When looking closely at *View from Theo's apartment*, one can see how

Van Gogh experimented with pointillism: the work is almost entirely made up of small dots, with lines being reserved for the contours of the houses.

This painting shows the view from the apartment shared by Van Gogh and Theo at 54, Rue Lepic, in the famous district of Montmartre.

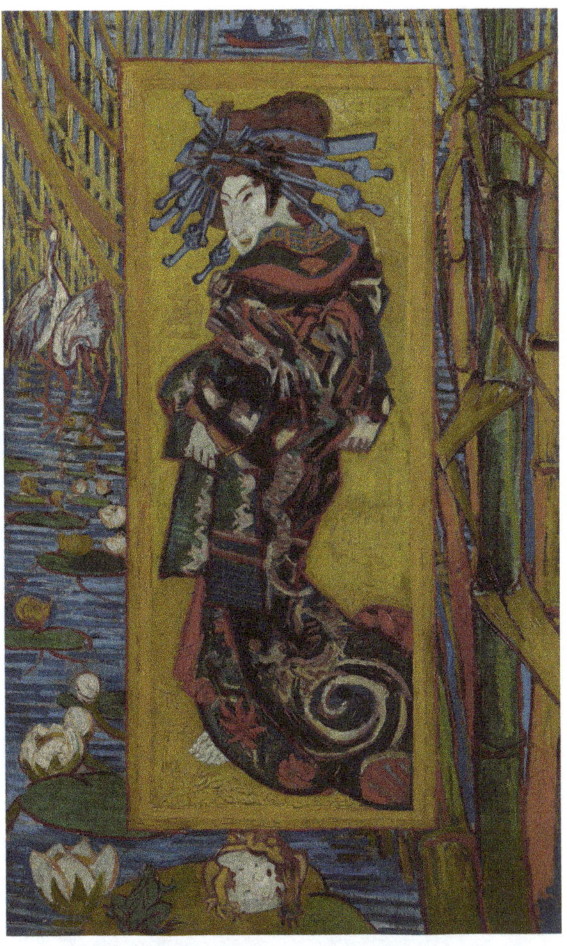

Vincent van Gogh, Courtesan (after Eisen), oil on canvas, October - November 1887

Van Gogh was fond of Japanese art, admiring the bright colors, clear contours and manner of composition. In *Courtesan*, he copied a portrait of a geisha from the cover of the *Paris Illustré* magazine. A geisha was a high-class courtesan who sometimes offered sexual favors.

In the background, Van Gogh has painted bamboo, frogs, canes and a small boat. The animals in particular were meant as a joke: the French words for crane ('grue') and frog ('grenouille') were also nicknames for a prostitute.

Bamboo frames the central image, magnified and placed in the foreground in a typically Japanese composition. Further back is a pond revealing small animals and lotus flowers dotted around the painting. In the work below, you can see another example of this type of composition.

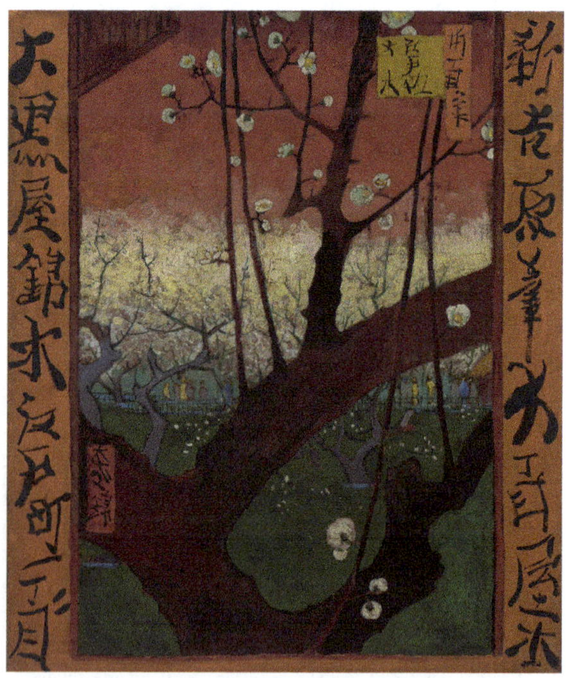

Vincent van Gogh, Flowering plum orchard (after Hiroshige), oil on canvas, October - November 1887

Van Gogh's japonaiserie also becomes clear in this painting of a garden. Like the bamboo in the image above, the tree is placed prominently in the foreground of this composition.

Close observation of the piece reveals a combination of styles, including the aforementioned Japanese composition which is combined with the impressionist brushstrokes of the blossoms in the background.

The borders are decorated with Japanese characters. Van Gogh was oblivious to their meaning, but copied the shapes simply liking the way they looked. The characters are actually an advertisement for a house up for a sale - including an address!

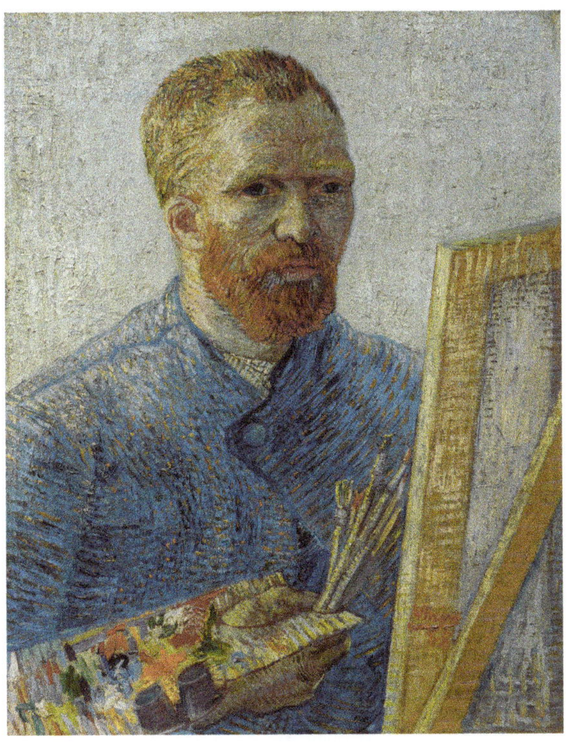

Vincent van Gogh, Self-portrait as a painter, oil on canvas, December 1887 - February 1888

Van Gogh painted many self-portraits. This was not out of vanity, but lack of money: instead of spending the little money he had on models, he bought a small mirror.

In this painting, he confidently portrays himself as an artist with his tools. Though many of his self-portraits are rather unrefined, this one is worth a closer look since it is very detailed.

This becomes clear in the number of colors he mixed to paint his hair and eyes. Van Gogh must have been pleased with the result; he confidently signed the painting at the lower right.

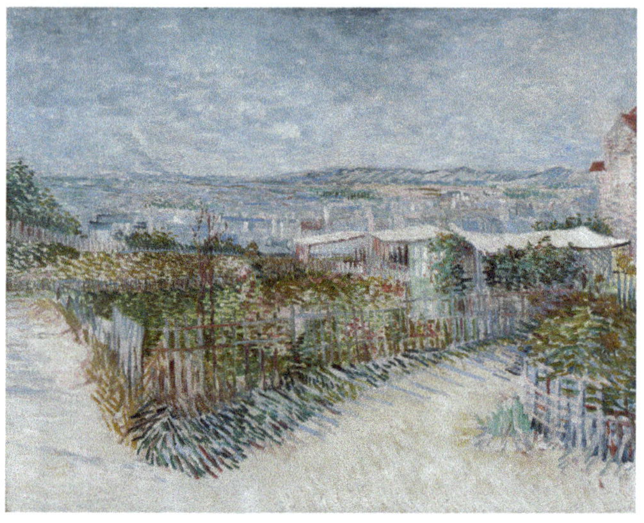

Vincent van Gogh, Montmartre: Behind the Moulin de la Galette, oil on canvas, July 1887

Impressionist painters aimed to portray the first impressions of the eye. This had to be done quickly, before the movement of the sun altered the light of the landscape. Therefore, impressionist paintings were often produced very quickly, resulting in a sketch-like appearance.

This painting is an example of Van Gogh experimenting with this style. Impressionist painters did not mix their paint on the palette before applying it, instead mixing the colors *on* the canvas itself, producing a far more varied spectrum.

Evidence of this can be seen in the pink house to the right, which contrasts beautifully with the sky and sandy path.

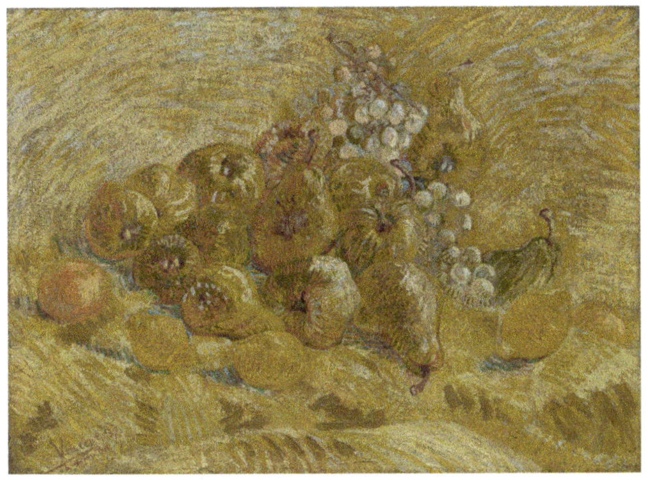

Vincent van Gogh, Quinces, lemons, pears and grapes, oil on canvas, October 1887

In Paris Van Gogh made various still lifes. This still life combining grapes, pears and lemons, one can make out the many influences on Van Gogh. The impressionist effect is immediately visible in the depiction of the fruit: the shadows emphasizing the shapes are not black, but in yellow, orange and white. The background clashes with the subject of the painting in its completely different rhythm of brushstrokes.

Japanese elements can be seen in the flatness of the perspective - the entire composition is made up of a large yellow color plane. Moreover, the frame is decorated with shapes that look like Japanese characters. Van Gogh dedicated this painting to the most important person in his life. Under his signature in the left bottom corner, he has written 'à mon frère Theo' - 'to my brother Theo'.

ARLES (1888 - 1889)

After spending just two years in Paris, Van Gogh yearned for the countryside. He chose to move to Arles, where the strong sunlight makes all colors deeper and brighter. There he rented part of a house, depicted in *The Yellow House*, and dreamed of setting up a commune for artists.

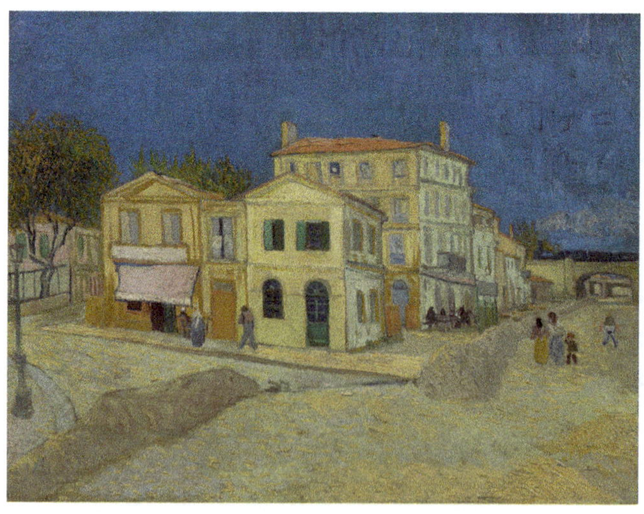

Vincent van Gogh, The Yellow House, oil on canvas, September 1888

The first painter to join Van Gogh in Arles was Paul Gauguin, an artist that he held in high esteem. Their collaboration lasted only nine weeks since they had many heated debates, ending with the infamous incident where Van Gogh cut off part of his earlobe. Interestingly, this was also the period when Van Gogh produced his greatest works.

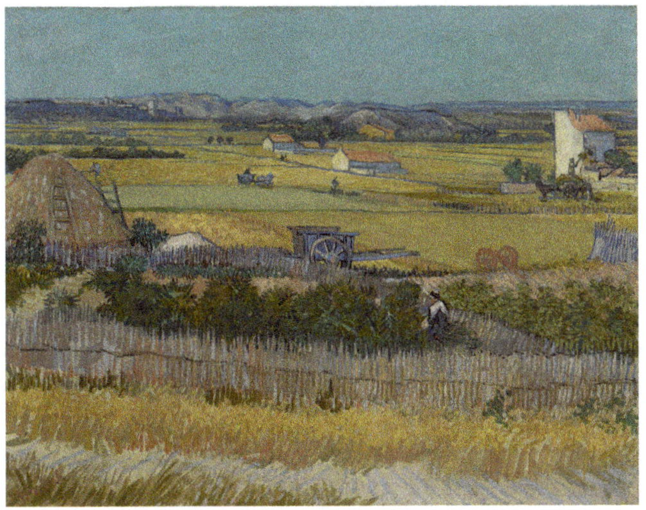

Vincent van Gogh, The Harvest at La Crau, oil on canvas, June 1888

This painting of a harvest is actually a Japanese-style French landscape. Comparing this work to the Parisian paintings of the geisha and the plum tree, strong similarities in both composition and color come to light.

Contrastingly, the cornfield is painted with impressionist dots and stripes. This is the magic of Van Gogh: he mixes different styles but the result is always genuinely his own.

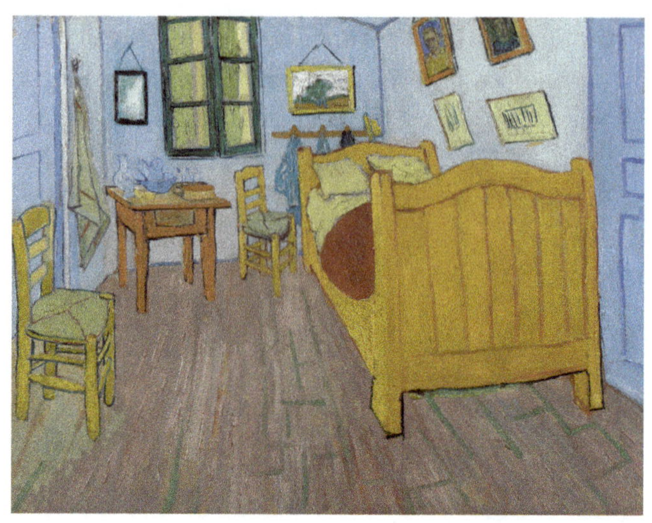

Vincent van Gogh, The Bedroom, oil on canvas, October 1888

Japanese influences are also visible in this famous painting of Van Gogh's bedroom. The perspective is not quite accurate, which was intentional.

In order to make it look more like a Japanese print, Van Gogh flattened the whole scene and left out all the shadows. You may recognize other Japanese elements like bright colors and clear contours.

It is clear from this painting that the painter's lifestyle was rather simple. Apart from the necessities, this sparse room does not include much, except for two simple chairs, a water bowl and paintings on the wall, including two portraits over his bed.

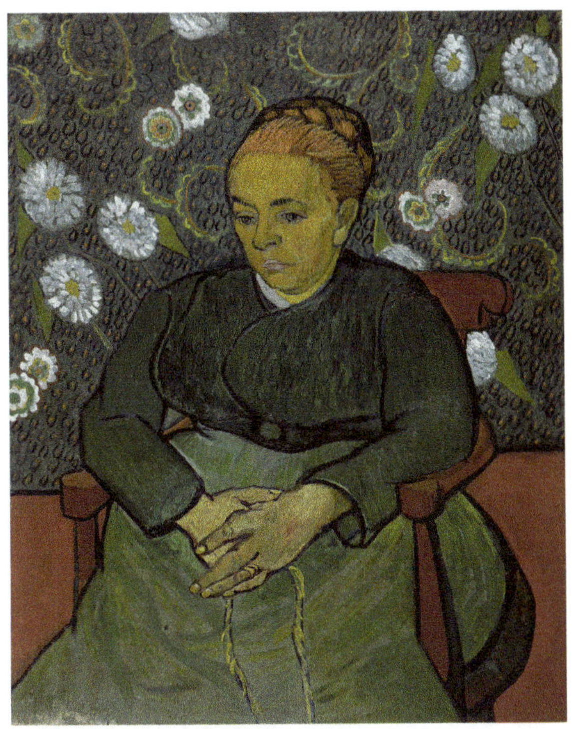

Vincent van Gogh, Augustine Roulin ("La berceuse"), oil on canvas, 1888

The woman portrayed here is Augustine Roulin, the wife of the postman Joseph Roulin, one of Van Gogh's closest friends in Arles. Her nickname 'la berceuse' means both 'lullaby' and 'babysitter' in French. This is alluded to by the cord in her hands, as it was used to rock the cradle while singing lullabies.

For Van Gogh, she was the ultimate symbol of comfort and motherhood. He planned to make a triptych using this painting as the middle panel, with pictures of sunflowers on either side. His intention was to combine motherly love with the beauty and power of nature.

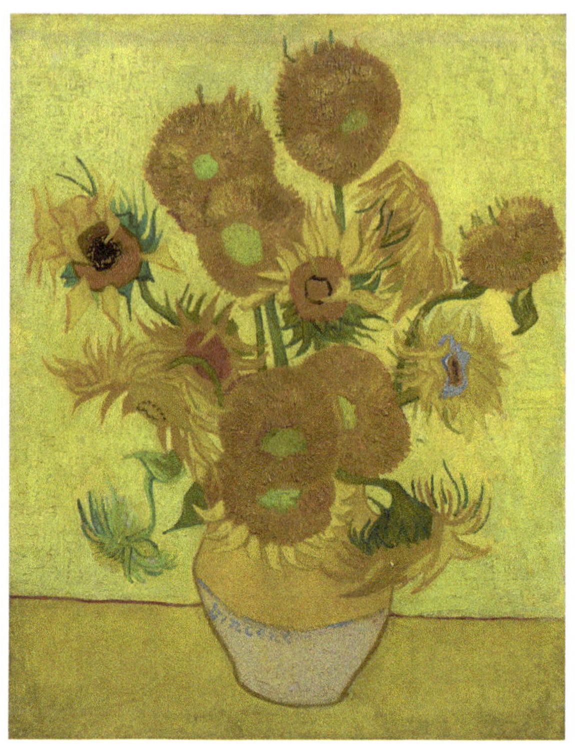

Vincent van Gogh, Sunflowers, oil on canvas, January 1889

Sunflower paintings are iconic of Van Gogh's *oeuvre*. In total, there are five different versions of this still life, and the Van Gogh Museum exhibits and owns the fifth and last of the series.

Van Gogh applied a vigorous energy to the painting of these flowers, and everything is imbued with a fierce yellow hue. The flowers are depicted through lumps of paint rather than brushstrokes.

Though originally conceived and designed as a side-panel for a painting that Van Gogh considered more important, the portrait of Augustine Roulin that is shown above, this painting is now perhaps the most famous of all of Van Gogh's works.

SAINT-RÉMY (1889 - 1890)

When Van Gogh was voluntarily admitted to the hospital in Saint-Rémy after cutting off his earlobe, he demanded an extra room to be able to work on his art. Beside his own paintings, he made copies of works that he loved.

Shown here is a Pietà, portraying the Virgin Mary mourning her son's death. This was made after a lithograph based on a painting by Eugène Delacroix (1798 - 1863).

By taking a closer look at the face of Jesus you may notice something familiar, as this is a self-portrait. Without a hint of arrogance, Van Gogh saw it as his way to identify with salvation and the end of suffering.

The painting actually is the result from a little accident. In his letter to Theo the artist wrote:

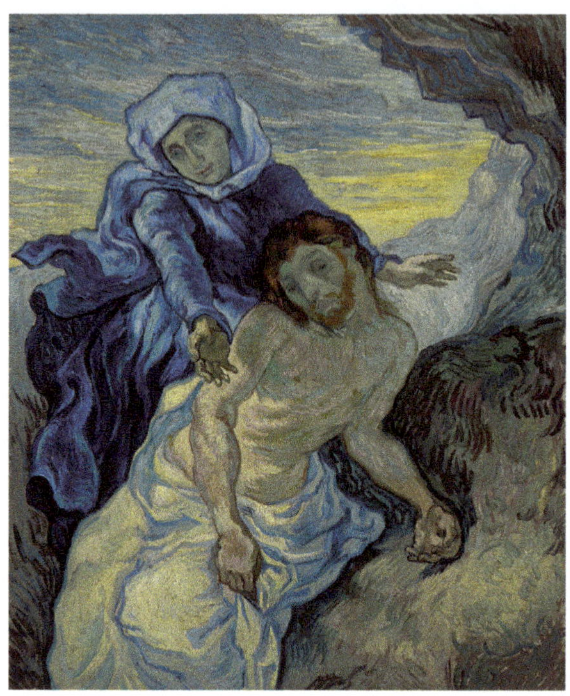

Vincent van Gogh, Pietà (after Delacroix), oil on canvas, September 1889

> “that lithograph of Delacroix, the Pietà, with other sheets had fallen into some oil and paint and got spoiled. I was sad about it – then in the meantime I occupied myself painting it, and you'll see it one day.”

The lithograph has survived, with the stain still visible.

After recovering from his illness in April 1890, Van Gogh worked on a series of flower still lifes. The subject of one these paintings is a bouquet of bright blue irises, set against a strong yellow background.

Compared to his sunflowers, this image is more balanced with regard to color, as the purple / blue flowers and green stems lend the painting a lighter and less bold tone.

You should see the painting as a study in color. Van Gogh planned to achieve a powerful color contrast. By placing the purple flowers against a yellow background, he made the decorative forms stand out strongly.

Interestingly, the red pigment in the flowers has faded. The irises were originally purple, and have now turned blue.

Van Gogh made two paintings of this joyous bouquet. In the still life (in the Metropolitan Museum of Art) he experimented with combining purple, pink and green.

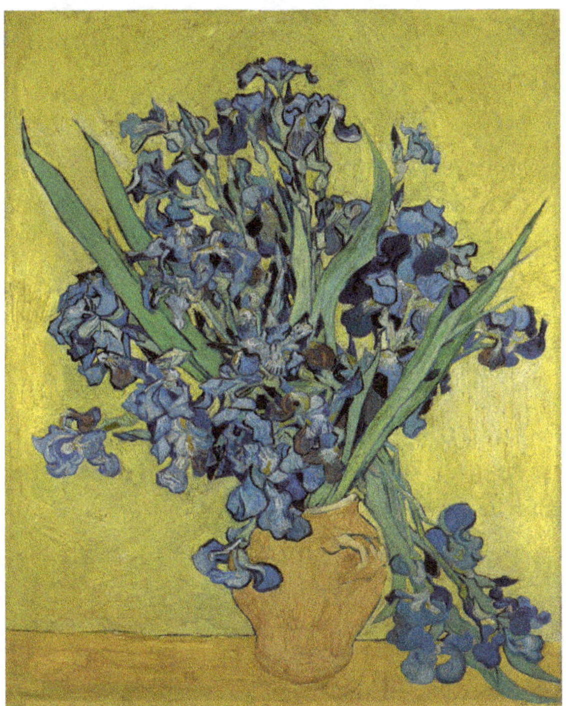

Vincent van Gogh, Irises, oil on canvas, May 1890

While in hospital in Saint-Rémy, Van Gogh painted many garden paintings where his use of color became almost autobiographic: in his own words, the combination of red, grey, green and thick black contours provoked anxiety.

The sky pictured in *Garden of the asylum* harbors a combination of bright colors in angled brushstrokes.

This has sometimes been explained as a result of the medication Van Gogh was taking, but remains open to interpretation.

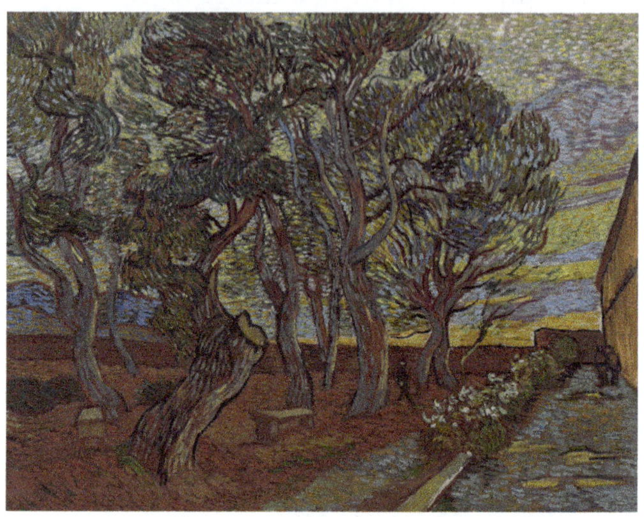

Vincent van Gogh, Garden of the Asylum, oil on canvas, December 1889

A tender expression of brotherly love is incorporated into this painting of almond blossoms. Theo van Gogh had married and wrote to the painter in 1890, telling him that their newborn son had been named 'Vincent'.

Bursting with pride, the artist set to work on a painting of blossoms on branches. Almond blossoms are symbols of new life as they bloom very early in the southern regions of France.

The artist's nephew Vincent would later become the founder of the Van Gogh Foundation, managing the collection of the Van Gogh Museum.

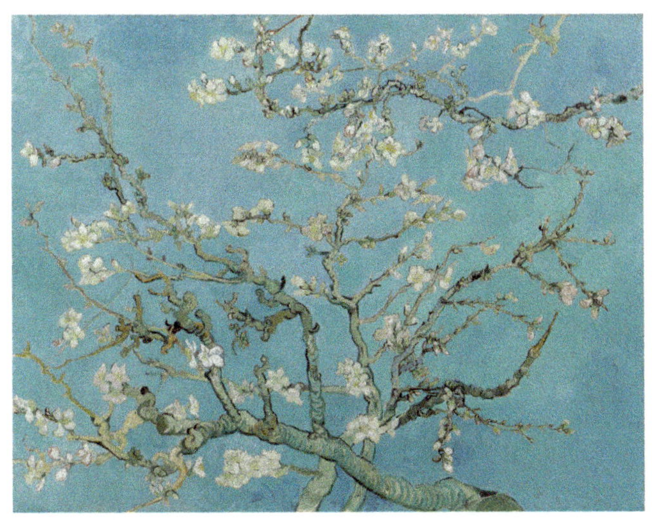

Vincent van Gogh, Almond Blossom, oil on canvas, February 1890

AUVERS-SUR-OISE (1890)

After leaving the hospital, Van Gogh went to live in Auvers-sur-Oise, a village close to Paris. It was here, in the last few months of his life, that he created a series of magnificent landscape paintings.

In *Wheatfield under Thunderclouds*, the clouds have become mere lumps of paint, and Van Gogh's style almost abstract.

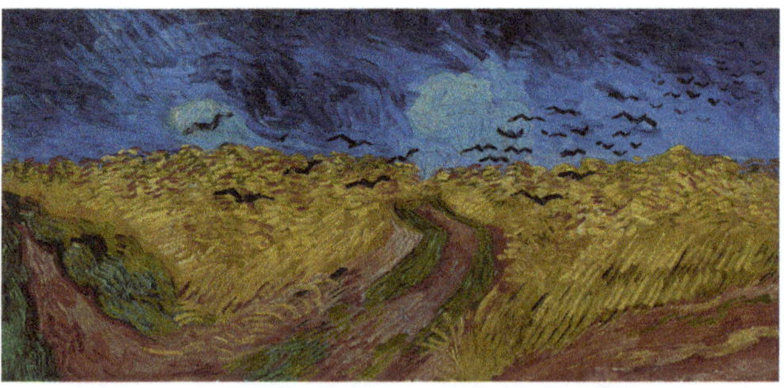

Vincent van Gogh, Wheatfield with Crows, oil on canvas, July 1890

This enigmatic landscape has long been regarded as Van Gogh's last painting. Though we now know that it is not his very last work, the sombre symbolism is difficult to overlook: the dark skies, the black crows, not to mention the ominous path leading nowhere.

The unfinished depiction of tree roots actually appears to be Van Gogh's last painting. Considering this painting was made only five years after *The Potato Eaters*, the development in such a short period of time is truly amazing.

Theo van Gogh's brother-in-law Andries Bonger alluded to the picture in a letter:

> 'The morning before his death, he had painted a sous-bois [forest scene], full of sun and life.'

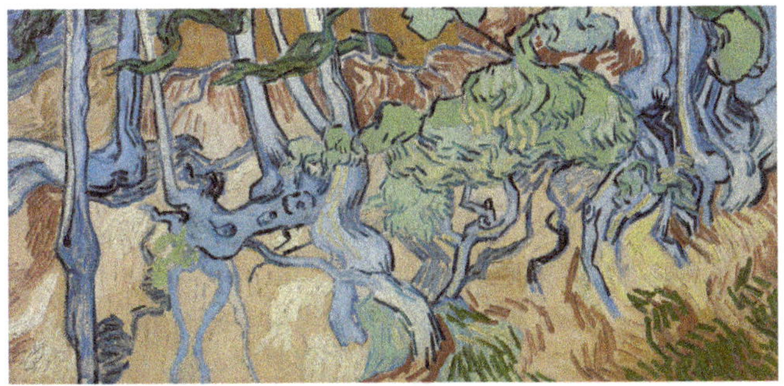

Vincent van Gogh, Tree Roots, oil on canvas, July 1890

OTHER ARTISTS IN THE COLLECTION

To provide visitors a better understanding of his full artistic development, the museum not only displays the artist's own work, but also works by influential contemporaries, as well as van Gogh's predecessors and followers. In the Rietveld building of the museum, you will find an extensive collection of paintings by artists related to Van Gogh in one way or another.

Characterised by bright colors and thick layers of paint, the works by the Dutch painter Kees van Dongen (1877 - 1968) were directly inspired by Van Gogh. They are in a style known as *Fauvisme,* or 'the style of wild animals'.

Fauvist artists aimed to work intuitively, with simple forms and bright colors. Van Dongen's favorite subject was the female body, which he called 'the most beautiful landscape there is'.

Portrayed here is Van Dongen's first wife, Guus Preitinger. Later in his career he became the portraitist of Parisian high society women like Brigitte Bardot.

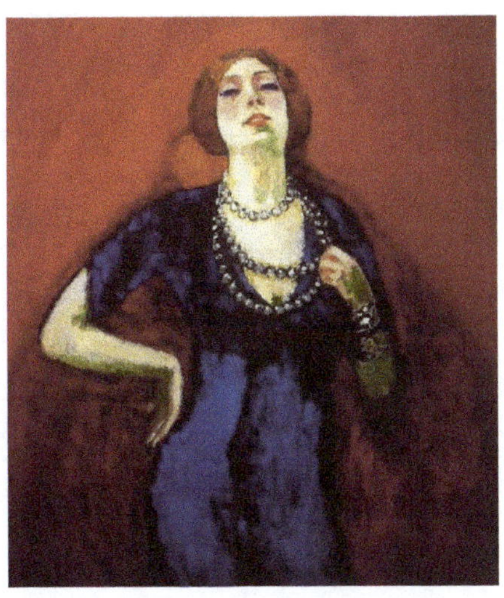

Kees van Dongen, Portrait of Guus Preitinger, the artist's wife, oil on canvas, 1911 © Kees van Dongen, De blauwe japon, 1911, c/o Pictoright Amsterdam 2017.

Kees van Dongen was popular as a portraitist of high society women. Rather sarcastically he observed that painting was the most beautiful of lies, and:

> "The essential thing is to elongate the women and especially to make them slim. After that it just remains to enlarge their jewels. They are ravished."

The self-portrait by Charles Laval (1862 - 1894) is the result of a deal the artist made with Van Gogh to exchange self-portraits.

Significantly, Laval did not place himself in the centre of the painting, but instead next to a window, offering us a view of the garden. Straight lines mark the window sills, yet the garden in the background appears more sketch-like.

Impressed with the painting, Van Gogh made a small drawing of it and included it in a letter to his brother Theo, describing it as 'very self-assured, very distinguished'.

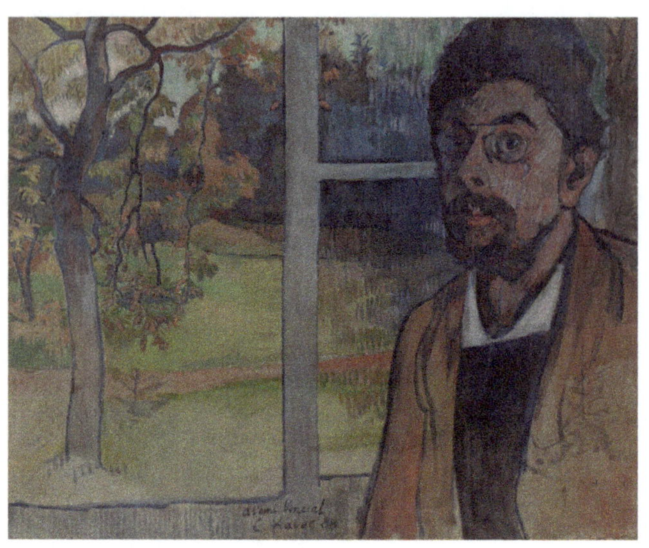

Charles Laval, Self-portrait, oil on canvas, 1888

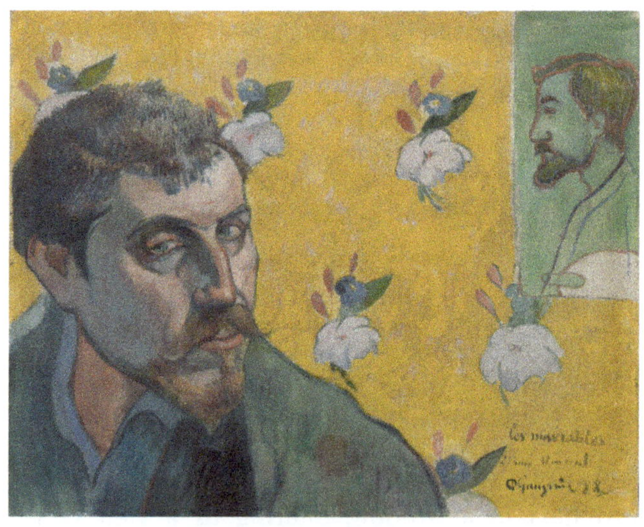

Paul Gauguin, Self-portrait with portrait of Émile Bernard (les misérables), oil on canvas, 1888

Paul Gauguin (1848 - 1903) portrayed himself in this painting as Jean Valjean, the protagonist in Victor Hugo's novel *'Les Misérables'*.

In Hugo's book, the hero is rejected by society but driven by inner convictions. As a painter in modern times, Gauguin considered himself to be in the same position, explaining his troubled expression, while the colors on the wall represent his purity as an artist.

In the background is a portrait of his close friend and colleague, Émile Bernard. Looking closely, you can also see Van Gogh in the bottom right corner, to whom this painting was dedicated.

1887 saw Paul Gauguin move to the Caribbean island of Martinique in an attempt to find inspiration in unspoiled surroundings. Holding a romantic view of life, he considered the natives of the island to be pure and noble savages with a direct connection to nature. This appealed to Gauguin as he sought spontaneity and authenticity.

Working in Martinique, he developed a new way of working with color. Yet for some art critics, the display of blue faces, green dogs, and purple trees was just 'evil'.

Gauguin loved the movements of the native women:

> "Their gestures are quite extraordinary; their hands play an important role, in harmony with the swaying of their hips."

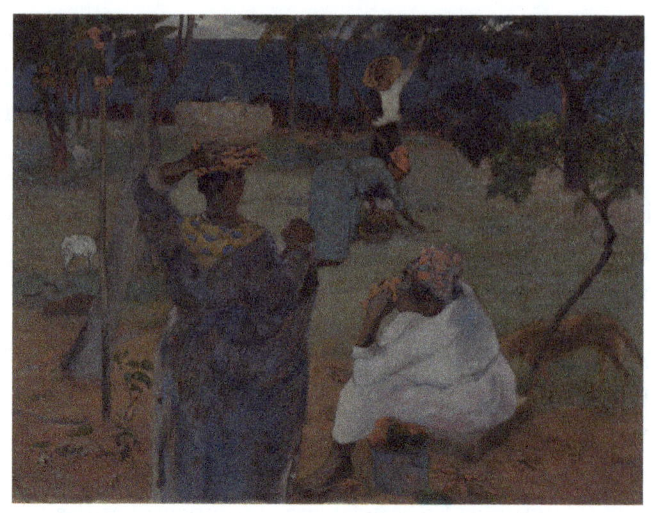

Paul Gauguin, The Mango trees, Martinique, oil on canvas, 1887

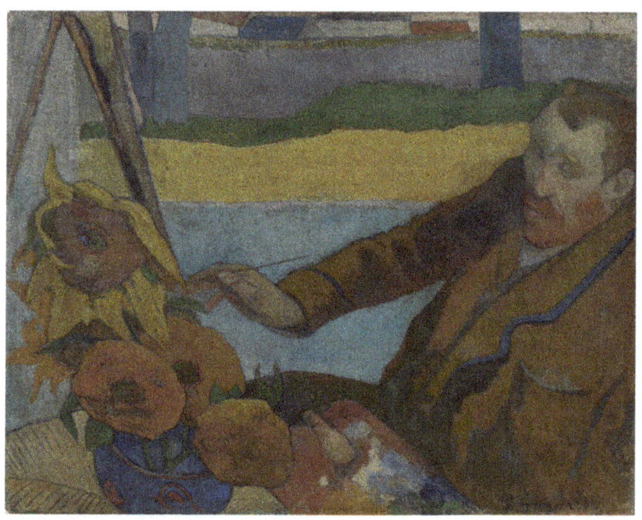

Paul Gauguin, Vincent van Gogh painting Sunflowers, oil on canvas, 1888

In *Vincent van Gogh painting Sunflowers* Gauguin painted his friend working on his famous sunflowers. Gauguin worked from the imagination, since the flowers were not in season; the painting was executed in December. This was one of the main areas of contention for the two artists: Van Gogh preferred to work from life while Gauguin used his powers of imagination.

When Van Gogh first saw the picture he was not pleased. He felt his friend had depicted him as a madman, but softened his view later on. He wrote to Theo:

> "My face has lit up after all a lot since, but it was indeed me, extremely tired and charged with electricity as I was then."

Flower still lifes became very popular in the 19th century. Without the obligation to tell a story or capture a likeness, the painter was free to experiment with shapes and colors.

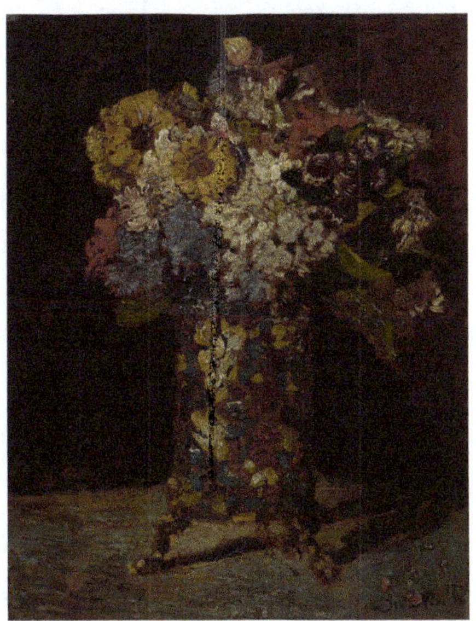

Adolphe Monticelli, Vase with flowers, oil on panel, circa 1875

When Theo van Gogh bought *Vase with flowers* by Adolphe Monticelli (1824 - 1886), his brother was ecstatic; he found the bright colors and the use of dots and stains instead of brushstrokes very inspiring. He asked his friends to buy him flowers, and then made a series of still lifes with the same composition.

In the 19th century, Jean François Millet (1814 - 1875) was at the forefront of a small but significant artistic revolution. Millet was the first to treat peasants as the subject in painting.

Before him, artists would regard them as picturesque elements in the background, no more important than animals, clouds and haystacks. Van Gogh admired Millet for his approach, and copied some of his works whilst being treated at the hospital in Saint-Rémy. During his stay in Saint-Rémy Van Gogh received a series of prints from Theo after paintings by Jean-François Millet. He 'translated' the black-and-white print into paintings in color. Below the Millet you will find one of these paintings by Van Gogh.

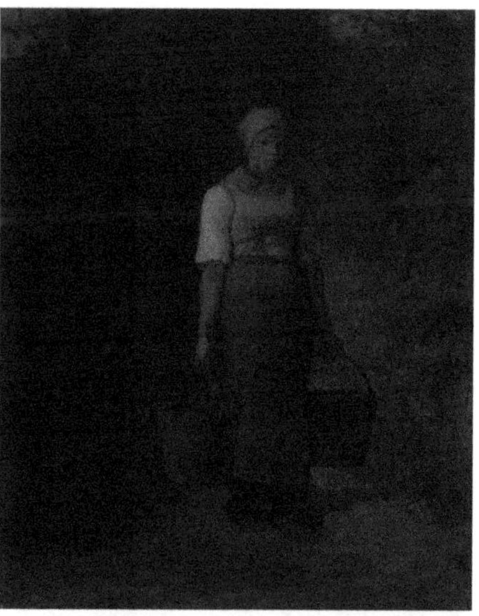

Jean François Millet, Girl carrying water, oil on canvas, 1855 - 1860

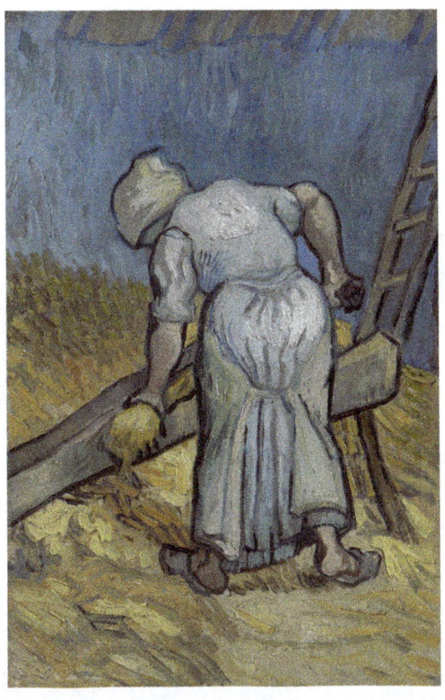

Vincent van Gogh, Peasant Woman bruising flax, oil on canvas, 1889

Due to his fondness for depictions of rural life, the works of the French painter Léon Augustin Lhermitte (1844 - 1925) interested Van Gogh greatly.

> 'I am too preoccupied by Lhermitte this evening to be able to talk of other things'.

The painting shows a group of farmers resting and repairing their tools. Though the scene appears informal, it is carefully staged - one can draw a circle to around the heads of the people portrayed, forming the centre of the composition. The horizon is high, allowing a gaze into the distance.

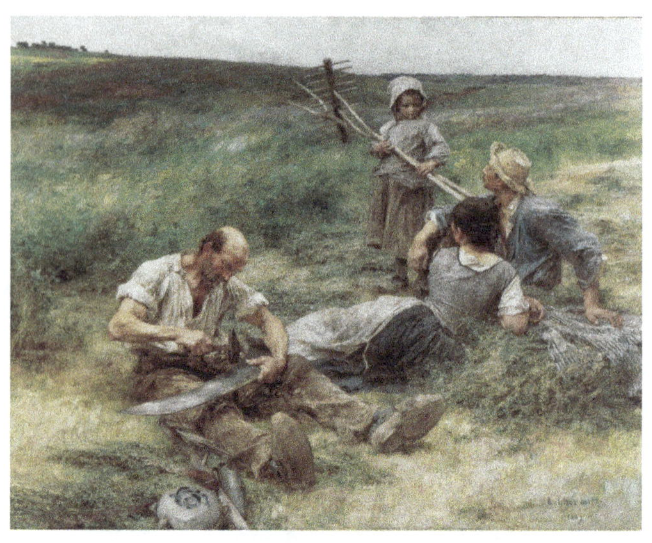

Léon-Augustin Lhermitte, Haymaking, oil on canvas, 1887

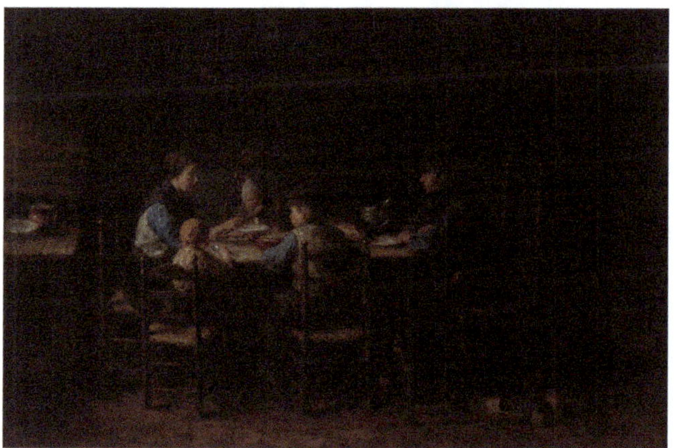

Jozef Israëls, Peasant Family at the table, oil on canvas, 1882

The painting of *Peasant Family at the table* by Jozef Israëls (1824 - 1911) is often shown with *The Potato Eaters* by Van Gogh.

Israëls was one of the most popular representatives of the Dutch so-called 'Hague School', whose painters focused on landscapes and the lives of farmers and fishermen.

This scene was a direct inspiration for Van Gogh, a realistic but sentimental portrayal with touching light effects and soft colors.

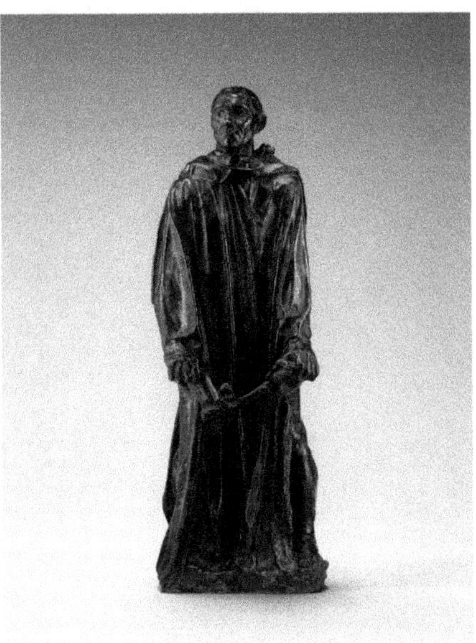

Auguste Rodin, Jean d'Aire from Burghers of Calais, patinated bronze, 1884

In 1884, the French sculptor, Auguste Rodin (1840 - 1917) received a commission to create a group of statues as a monument for the *Burghers of Calais*. These legendary figures attempted to save their city from pillaging by the English in 1346 by offering themselves as hostages and handing over the key to the city.

One of the statues of this group is in the Van Gogh Museum, and represents the burgher Jean d'Aire, showing his raw features and humble clothes. A grim expression disfigures his face: he is about to leave the city, in all likelihood facing death.

When exhibited, the monument was shown without a pedestal, allowing the viewer to feel the suffering and humiliation whilst walking through the group of statues.

Gustave Caillebotte, View seen through a balcony, oil on canvas, 1880

Like Van Gogh, the French painter Gustave Caillebotte (1848 - 1894) experimented with Japanese elements. In this painting, the wrought-iron balcony dominates the foreground while Avenue Hausman is placed to the back, with people and horses shown merely as shadowy figures. Rather than the view on the Boulevard, the cast-iron curly pattern of the balcony is the actual subject of this modern painting.

The landscape illustrated below is painted by Camille Pissarro (1831 - 1903) who was a major influence on Van Gogh. Using dots, stripes and bright colors, it shows the haymaking in August. It is easy to draw comparisons when looking at Van Gogh's *Square St. Pierre*, painted in Paris (see Paris section). The other artist was so important to Van Gogh that he was nicknamed 'Father Pissarro'.

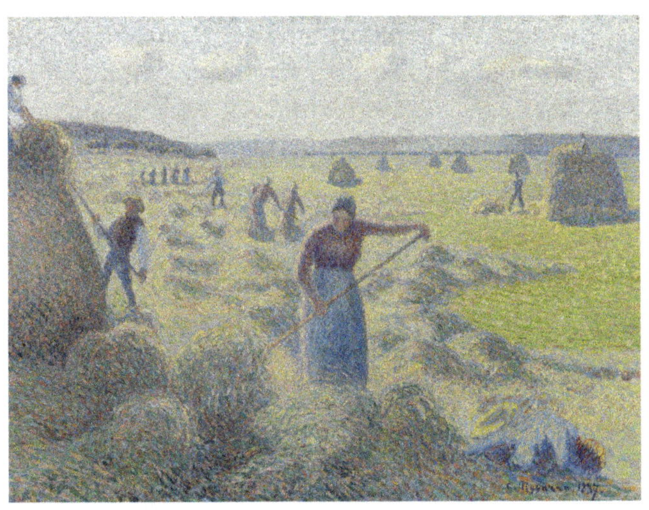

Camille Pissarro, Haymaking, Éragny, oil on canvas, 1887

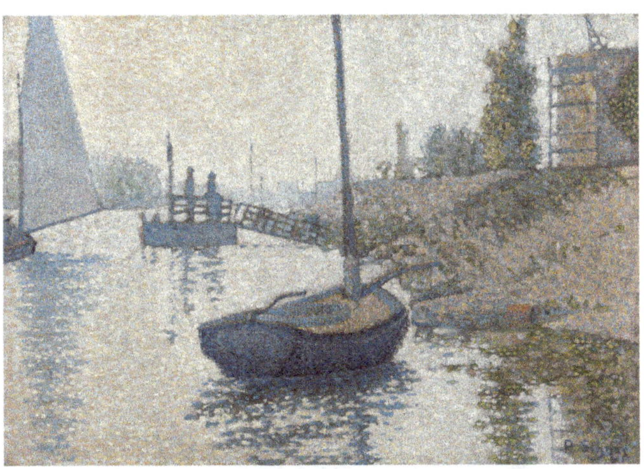

The "Ponton de la Félicité" at Asnières (Opus no. 143) Paul Signac, 1886

The *"Ponton de la Félicité" at Asnières (Opus no. 143)* is the first pointillist painting by Signac in the Van Gogh Museum, filling an important gap in its collection. Paul Signac painted this in 1886 on the banks of the Seine near Asnières.

Van Gogh and Signac met in Paris in 1887. Both artists often went to

Asnières to paint on the banks of the river Seine. Van Gogh admired by Signac's free application of the pointillist technique, and his use of bright, complementary colors. Although Van Gogh himself only made a couple of works using a strictly pointillist style, this manner of painting became the basis of his characteristic style, which features expressive dashes and short lines of pure color placed next to one another.

With regard to Signac's influence on the development of Van Gogh's work, artist friend Emile Bernard said:

> "He [Van Gogh] was already in the process of 'changing his palette' and, acting on Signac's advice, was experimenting with a free form of divisionism."

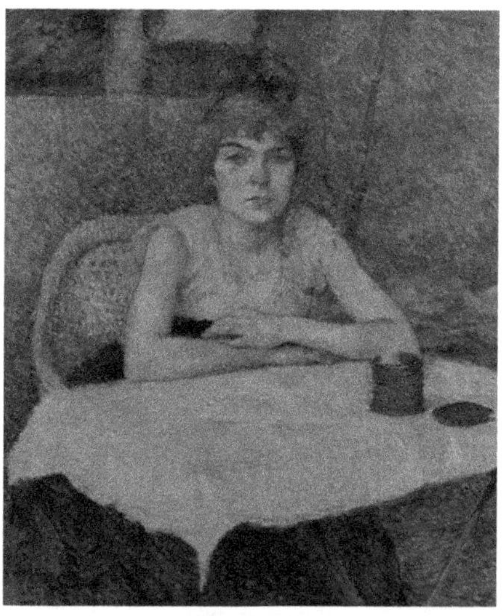

Henri de Toulouse-Lautrec, Young woman at a table, 'poudre de riz', oil on canvas, 1887

This woman has often been referred to as Suzanne Valadon, the mistress of Henri de Toulouse-Lautrec (1864 - 1901), a close friend of Van Gogh. It is not sure that it is her actually. The two artists met at the Atelier Cormon in Paris where both studied for a while.

The painting is called *Poudre de riz*, or 'rice powder', named after the red jar on the table containing make-up. Rice was used to achieve a pale complexion, a sign of beauty. When you are in the museum you will see that the paint surface is rather matt. Toulouse Lautrec used a blotting paper to remove the glossy oil from the paint, which was then diluted with turpentine. The technique was popular among modern painters.

On Van Gogh's recommendation Theo van Gogh bought *Poudre de riz* for their collection. Since he did not earn a penny with his own work, Van Gogh thought it was a good investment that they (i.e. Theo) would acquire works of art by their contemporaries and thus create their own collection of modern art. In this process Van Gogh acted at the advisor. All of these pictures can nowadays be seen at the Van Gogh museum.

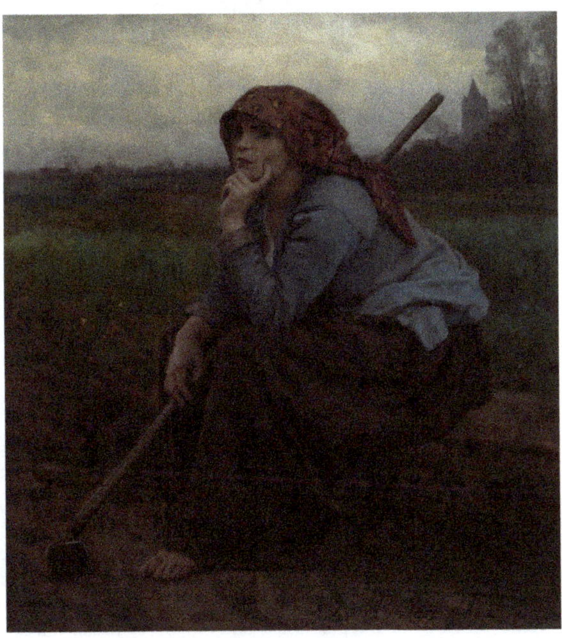

Jules Breton, Young peasant girl with a hoe, oil on canvas on panel, 1882

Van Gogh admired Millet and also the French painter and poet, Jules

Breton (1827 - 1905), both painters of rural scenes. Even though Breton was a realist painter, this image betrays a hint of sentimentalism. The peasant girl stares out of the picture; her eyes are pensive and tones muted. Van Gogh was no enemy of the sentimental, stating that 'one must have imaginative power and sentiment while painting'. Like Van Gogh, Breton followed in the footsteps of painters with an interest in country life and realism, such as Jean-François Millet.

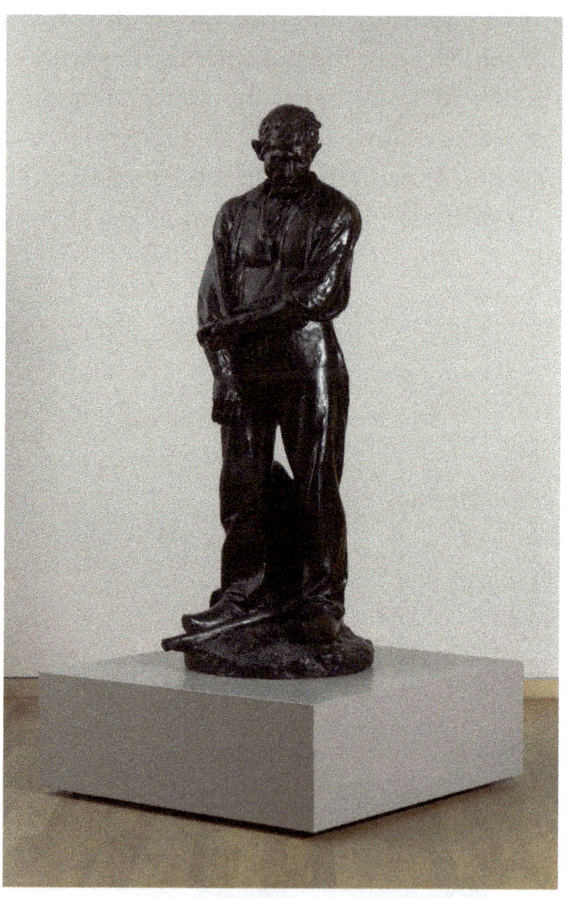

Aimé Jules Dalou, Tall peasant, bronze, 1898 - 99 (design circa 1899, cast 1902 - 1905)

This statue of a farmer rolling up his sleeves would have been very much to Van Gogh's taste. Like in *The Potato Eaters*, the subject is the hard-working common man, portrayed with dignity. The sculptor Aimé Jules Dalou (1838 - 1901) was a working-class hero. Born a laborer's son, he knew the hardships of ordinary people only too well. In his work, he gave these people a face.

Like Rodin's statue of Jean d'Aire, the statue of the tall peasant was part of a group of sculptures glorifying labor.

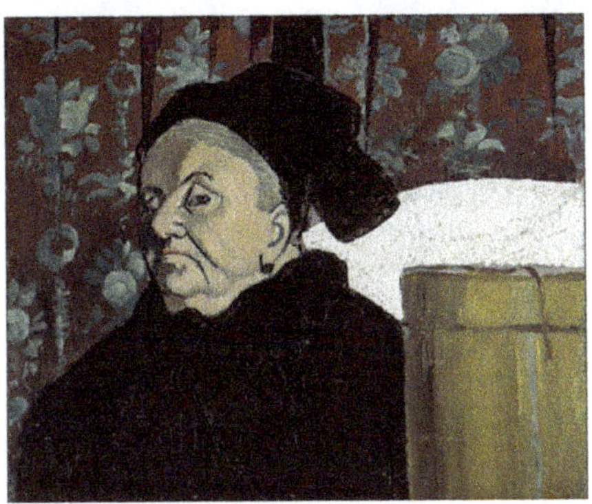

Émile Bernard, Portrait of his Grandmother, oil on canvas, 1887

While Van Gogh was supported, personally and financially, by his brother Theo, the French painter Émile Bernard (1868 - 1941) relied on his grandmother, Mrs. Bodin-Lallement, a lady who appears regularly in his paintings.

Like many other painters of his day, Bernard was influenced by Japanese art, as can be seen in the large planes of color, clear contours and magnified details in the foreground.

In his days as an assistant minister in England, Van Gogh often mentioned the paintings by the English artist George Henry Boughton (1833 - 1904) in his sermons. Van Gogh was especially enthusiastic about the work showing pilgrims setting out for Canterbury. He would often tell his congregation, 'life is a voyage towards God', and in this painting one can see pilgrims having their flasks filled with water as they are on their way to Canterbury.

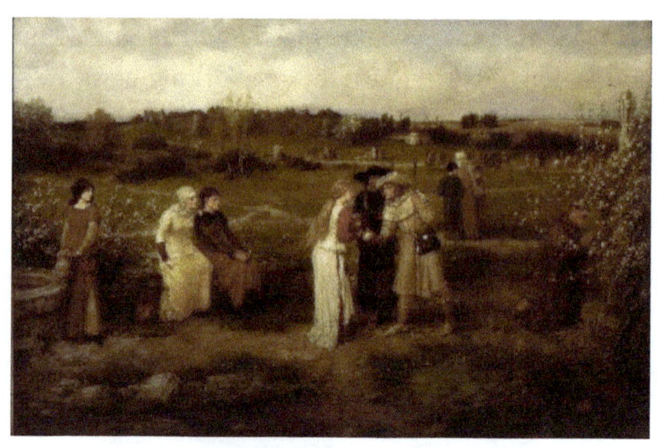

George Henry Boughton, Godspeed! Pilgrims setting out for Canterbury, oil on canvas, 1874

PRACTICAL INFORMATION

Time-slotted admission tickets regulate visitor distribution. The peaks and lows of visitor flows are less pronounced than they used to be, and visitors are distributed more evenly throughout the entire day. One in four visitors purchases a ticket online in advance.

Extended opening hours on Fridays (and in the summer months also on Saturdays) allow the museum to deal with the busy summer period. Often people are not aware of the fact that the museum is open on Friday until 10 pm, so that also may be a good time to visit.

If you wish to visit during the day, is advisable to go there between 9 am and 11 am, or after 3 pm.

Try to avoid the busiest times which are between 11 am and 3 pm.

Please note: last admission is 30 minutes before closing time.

You can order entrance tickets online for direct access at your preferred time and date. Tickets are available four months in advance.

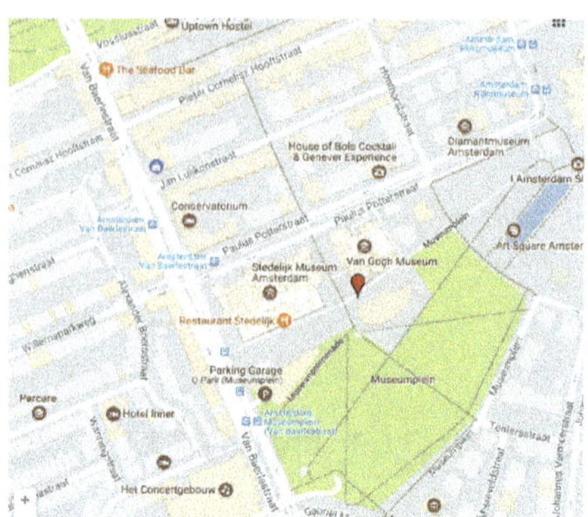

Map of Museumplein Amsterdam

FURTHER READING

The series **Amsterdam Museum Guides** consist of accessible museum guides. They are a great way to fully prepare your visit to Amsterdam.

Rijksmuseum Amsterdam is the essential guide to the highlights of the Rijksmuseum in Amsterdam. The guide is fully up-to-date and contains many color images of the paintings and objects in this greatest treasure trove of Holland. Since the museum contains too many works of art to digest in one day, it is best to concentrate on its highlights so you can maximize your viewing experience.

The Anne Frank House Amsterdam is a brief guide to the world famous hiding place of the Jewish girl Anne Frank during the Second World War. And the Hermitage Amsterdam provides a brief introduction to this satellite of the St Petersburg Museum.

Should you wish to read all of them, they have now been compiled into one practical guide: Things To Do in Amsterdam: Museums.

We have made a selection for you of the most important Amsterdam Museums. Unfortunately the Stedelijk Museum could not be included in this series of museumguides for Amsterdam museums because of copyright on modern art, but the museum is worthwhile a visit.

COLOPHON

Title: Van Gogh Museum Amsterdam. Highlights of the Collection

Authors: Marko Kassenaar & Liesbeth Heenk

Publisher: Amsterdam Publishers, The Netherlands

ISBN 13 paperback: 9789492371379

ISBN 13 ebook: 9789492371386

www.ingramcontent.com/pod-product-compliance
Ingram Content Group UK Ltd.
Pitfield, Milton Keynes, MK11 3LW, UK
UKHW021839270726
14058UKWH00002B/240